LEDI

LEDI

KIM TRAINOR

BOOK*HUG 2018

The production of this book was made possible through the generous assistance of the Canada Council for the Arts and the Ontario Arts Council. Book*hug also acknowledges the support of the Government of Canada through the Canada Book Fund and the Government of Ontario through the Ontario Book Publishing Tax Credit and the Ontario Book Fund.

Book*hug acknowledges the land on which it operates. For thousands of years it has been the traditional land of the Huron-Wendat, the Seneca, and most recently, the Mississaugas of the Credit River. Today, this meeting place is still the home to many Indigenous people from across Turtle Island, and we are grateful to have the opportunity to work on this land.

Library and Archives Canada Cataloguing in Publication
Trainor, Kim, 1970-, author
    Ledi / Kim Trainor. -- First edition.

Poems.
Issued in print and electronic formats.
ISBN 978-1-77166-447-9 (softcover).
ISBN 978-1-77166-448-6 (HTML).
ISBN 978-1-77166-449-3 (PDF)
ISBN 978-1-77166-450-9 (Kindle)

    I. Title.

PS8639.R355L43 2018   C811'.6   C2018-904267-2
                                              C2018-904268-0

PRINTED IN CANADA

In the crook of the Lady's knee was a red cloth case containing a small hand mirror of polished metal with a deer carved into its wooden back. Beads wound around her wrist, and more tattoos decorated her wrist and thumb. She was tall, about five feet six. She had doubtless been a good rider, and the horses in the grave were her own. As we worked, the fabric gradually revived around her limbs, softening the outline of her legs, the swell of her hip. And somehow, in that moment, the remains became a person. She lay sideways, like a sleeping child, with her long, strong aristocratic hands crossed in front of her. Forgive me, I said to her.

—Natalia Polosmak

Every morning I wake at dawn and watch the blue light seep
through cracks and blinds, like water all around.

It trickles through sockets, into my mouth,
my throat, until I am filled with light and can see
the cage of bones, damp heart,
dark venous blood at wrist and breast as it scatters
through cross-hatched transparent skin.

I am clear in this tidal light.

And then it goes, leaving ligaments and thews strewn
like dried grasses. Butterflied lungs.
A residue of salt in the scraped hollows.

ॐ

I.
WRENCHED
FROM THE
COLD EARTH

3 May. I have come to the university to read about Ledi, the technique used to excavate her burial cairn. The steppe is said to have a *glacial memory.* Her grave was a lens of ice focussing dark shadows.

It melted slowly in the weak sunlight. To speed the process, they hauled buckets of lake water to the grave and heated these with a blowtorch. Bailed out the meltwater each morning. Plagued by mosquitoes and the stench of rotting horsemeat. Then switched to enamel cups of heated water as her body emerged.

A jawbone. A shoulder, fur peeled back
to reveal a griffin tattooed on her flesh.

The body emerged from the ice like a temple rubbing.

Spring everywhere underfoot—snowdrops, cyclamen, oxeye
    daisies, wild garlic.

CR

3 May. I have been inaccurate. They began with pickaxes and iron bars, probing the ice as it melted. Then buckets of heated lake water. What had been frozen solid for millennia thawed overnight. When the hot water made contact with slaughtered horse flesh, it formed a *meaty broth*. The archaeologist's dog drank this *with no negative effects.*

☞

The burial chamber of birch skin and larch swells with winter rains
and snowmelt trickling down two thousand years.

Grave goods lift and settle over time.

Here an iron knife skewers a piece of mutton.

Here coriander fruits rest in a stone dish beside the larch casket.

Clasped in silk and fur, tattooed griffin perched on her shoulder.

Inked bracelet. In the crook of her knee,
a red-sheathed mirror she used to summon the dead.

Blue above, and flowers, and steppe-meadow grasses.

☙

At 10:35 on Monday morning, July 19, something emerged through the ragged edges of a hole in the ice—a bare jawbone but with the flesh of a cheek intact. That afternoon a shoulder appeared, covered by a brilliant blue tattoo of a magnificent griffin-like creature.

☙

3 May. I stop reading. Look out at the May sunlight. The campus is empty. Paths strewn with cherry petal. Green flicker of alder. As I have grown older, I have grown more alone. I have lost friends.

My first lover took his own life. We met at the university radio station. I fell in love with his voice. We were together seven years.

He drifted from me in the last year of his life. Then I met someone else and moved to Montreal. I didn't know for many days that he had died. I don't know where his ashes are scattered.

His voice escapes the earth's atmosphere and travels forever through space, growing fainter and fainter.

I can barely hear him anymore.

ᛞ

For the Siberian peoples larches, unlike cedars, were
regarded as sacred trees just as birch trees were. The Selkups
associated larches with the Sun and the Sky, with holy birds
such as eagles or cranes. It was believed that the crowns
of larch trees reached up to the heavens....This placing of
noble Pazyryks and certain of their children in closely sealed
sarcophagi made of hollowed-out larch trees can be seen as
a symbolic attempt to return them to the womb and prepare
them for rebirth...Burials on trees, inside tree trunks or tree-
stumps were designed to return the dead to the source of life.

Altai anemone, oxeye daisy, snow drop. Siberian barberry,
   holy wormwood.

୧୫

4 May. Once they had removed the cover of the larch casket—secured by six-inch-long bronze nails—they were ecstatic to find a solid block of ice. This meant the body within had not been disturbed.

Then the blue-lipped cups of lake water poured like a libation.

She lay exactly as she had been placed her last day on earth.

We had intercepted a suspended moment.

 CR

4 May. In our first year together, he tried to take his life. He ran into the forest surrounding the university and stayed there until it was night. He was afraid and didn't know what he was doing. He told me all this much later. He wanted to die. He didn't want to die. No one knew where he had gone.

I imagine him now in the forest's green dusk. Swordfern and dogwood. Bitter dock. The terror he feels knowing he must rip out his life, like a root from the soil.

I waited to hear news of him at my parents' house. A wooden clock on the mantelpiece hollowed out time.

I couldn't feel my arms. My arms had been taken from me.

I couldn't breathe. My breath had been taken from me.

When it grew dark, he ran out onto the highway, and was struck by a car.

 CR

She was prepared for a life after death.

The patho-anatomists felt that the most likely kind of dissection of the woman's body would have been a ventral one. All the organs and also the cartilaginous parts of the ribs and the breast-bone had been removed. The thoracic, abdominal and pelvic cavities had been filled with earth and thin roots of grasses.

Steppe fescue, couch grass, steppe oat, wild oat, spear grass.

CR

5 May. I saw him that night in intensive care. He was unconscious, hooked to an IV. Spare black hairs on his chest, his skin white as paper. A dark bruise like a fingerprint on the side of his nose. A wound in the soft flesh of his forearm. His mother tried to cover his chest with the green hospital gown, to hide his body from me.

ℭ℞

The slow bruise
of a woman's darkening
form deep-rooted

flowers sip—
tenacious, white-tipped
ghosts hungering

for her.

ଓ

5 May. I return to this moment. It is spring. He is alone in the forest. The spring light is like glass. He rests on a skin of bracken and moss. He absorbs the green dusk until he is heavy as earth. As the dark enters him, he decides it is time to go. His body leaves a print in the wet humus of salmonberry and salal. It leaves a sweet trace on his skin.

ᘓ

7 May. The Pazyryks classified their deaths.

A heavy death would be that of an elder, especially one who died in a dwelling, as their impurities were many, having lived a long life, and their attachments to the living were deep-rooted.

A light death would be that of a nursing child, a youth under the age of fifteen, a suicide. These were more likely to go freely into the next world, to not haunt the living.

I am not so sure.

Meadow ragwort and Seguière's pink, campion and iris root. Blue-flowered thyme and aconite and holy wormwood.

 CR

The mortal shell of the deceased came to contain what could be seen as symbolizing the world that surrounded the nomad: earth and grass from the pastures, the coats of the beasts that grazed there—all this the deceased would carry off with him on his journey to the 'heavenly' pastures.

Couch grass, yellow oat grass, feather grass, cat's paw. Cyclamen, campion, Iris ruthenica.

ଔ

7 May. Of all the accounts of her, I am most touched by the description of her hollowed body *filled with earth and thin roots of grasses.*

All flesh is grass, and all the goodliness thereof is as the flower of the field.

℞

Hear the click of beads at her wrist,
taste burnt coriander

on the wind. She is not here.
Only these white flowers

like moths that draw light
to them, their dry form.

ⵣ

I believe that thoughts and ideas do not vanish, that they still exist in the layers of the atmosphere that blanket the earth.

II.
INTEGUMENT

12 May. When Ledi died, her body was scoured of everything wet and soft, then replaced with earth and grasses. She was dressed in a tunic of wild tussah silk and hip-length white felt stockings, wrapped in a blanket of marten fur and placed in a casket of hollowed larch. Her people ate a last meal of mutton and koumiss at her side, and burned a dish of coriander. The grave was closed with earth and a kurgan of stones raised to mark its location.

This would have taken many days.

Grass grows slowly over the grave. Above the steppe the endless sky.

Two thousand years pass.

◌

Herodotus, on the burial customs of the Scythians: *the belly is slit open, cleaned out, and filled with various aromatic substances, crushed galingale, parsley-seed, and anise; it is then sewn up again and the whole body coated over with wax. In this condition it is carried in a wagon to a neighbouring tribe within the Scythian dominions, and then on to another, taking the various tribes in turn; and in the course of its progress the people who successively receive it, follow the custom of the Royal Scythians and cut a piece from their ears, shave their hair, and thrust arrows through their left hands. On each stage of the journey those who have already been visited join the procession, until at last the funeral cortège, after passing through every part of the Scythian dominions, finds itself at last at the place of burial amongst the Gerrhi, the most northerly and remote of Scythian tribes.*

CS

13 May. Every description I have read of Ledi's excavation differs, in chronology, in detail, in tenor.

Her left shoulder juts through the ice. They pick off the disintegrating fur, peel the silk caul of her tunic.

For the first time in two thousand years her skin is touched by human hands and sunlight.

She begins immediately to decay.

☙

In various light she resembles:

chert

leather

peeled bark

a cave painting of ochre and soot

dirt

‰

14 May. The techniques used to excavate Ledi were called *barbaric.* Awls and pickaxes. Cupfuls of heated lake water.

First glimpse of her. She lies on her side, as if asleep. A jawbone protrudes through the ice. A cheekbone with flesh intact.

Her spine has worked its way through her stomach.

☙

She appears on the page of my notebook like a temple rubbing—

Press hard. Antler tips pierce her left clavicle.
A bracelet of soot. Press harder. Thin veins
show through paper. All the small bones. Blank patches
where the body gapes over straw-filled cavities.

Use the flat of the charcoal to draw out the skull's smooth
  contours.

႙

15 May. I have been thinking of what it means to be alone. He once told me that when he talked to people they didn't really hear him. His words passed through their bodies like subatomic particles without touching them, leaving no trace at all.

☙

In various light:

charred meat

kindling

a clump of roots

meadow grass

ଔ

X-rays are taken of the bones that slip from her remaining flesh.

She is arranged on a table in milk-white translucencies.

She is trying to raise herself up on one elbow to get away—see the tilt
of her left shoulder, her head tipped to the right, the mouth
open as if calling out. Her arms,
folded, cradle her belly, knees bent.

See the long closed finger bones.

ᆭ

Her skin tells a story—

a deer with a griffin's beak
and the antlers of an ibex
flower at her shoulder

a smaller deer chases her wrist

stains on her fingers

soot needle tracks.

C３

With tattoo, "the body multiplies, additional organs and subsidiary selves are created; spirits, ancestors, rulers and victims take up residence in an integument which begins to take on a life of its own."

The skin bears an *ancestral imprintation.* The skin is the first boundary, first place of contact, with the past, with one's tribe, with another.

ଓଃ

17 May. Isn't our skin like a photograph? It carries the trace of others. It develops in time. A scraped knee. A tiny scar below the lip. Fingerprints of a lover's grasp smudged blue, then ochre.

ଔ

17 May. It has become instinct for me now to turn away from other people, to climb more deeply into my body, as if it were a cave, and crouch here, watching from a safe distance.

The thoracic, abdominal, and pelvic cavities had been filled with earth and thin roots of grasses. All that had survived of the right arm was part of the forearm and the palm of the hand...The left arm had been preserved quite well, apart from one breakage near the joint. At the place where that break had occurred some of the filling was visible—grass and roots.

ॐ

17 May. There is no blood in me.

☙

Who might the young woman buried in Burial-mound I of the Ak-Alakh 3 burial-ground actually be?

❧

19 May. It has been so hot this May. I lie down in the dark in a thin T-shirt. Curvature of rib, hollowed clavicles, hip bones. When I lie on my side my knees scrape, bone on bone. When it grows cool in the night, I wrap myself in a white sheet.

How hard it is to emerge.

☙

21 May. When her body had at last been freed from the ice, they lifted her onto a canvas stretcher. She will always lie this way, her raised left shoulder with its elaborate tattoos, head tipped back, knees bent, fetal. She is bound in gauze and carried to a makeshift shelter.

Wildflowers everywhere underfoot—snowdrops, cyclamen, oxeye daisies, wild garlic.

Overhead—the steppe's depthless blue.

III.
INVENTORY

A hollowed out larch casket, curving gently, like a cradle.

Six-inch-long bronze nails.

Sacrificed horses, with chestnut manes. Killed by a blow to the skull with a small axe called a *chekan*.

Their partially digested stomach contents—grass, pine needles, twigs.

The sough of the wind.

A tunic of wild tussah silk, yellow with maroon piping, rinsed out with lake water.

A blanket of marten fur.

A black cotton T-shirt.

A headdress with carvings of eight gold-painted cats and a pair of swans.

Shoulder bag with wallet and keys.

A small stone dish with remnants of coriander seeds—a medicinal herb to ease the lady's journey—lay beside the headdress. A pool of black substance, perhaps hair-dye, was beneath her skull.

Tuesday morning. The sun's vertebrae burning on the walls of this room.

In *The Histories* Herodotus writes: *As regards war, the Scythian custom is for every man to drink the blood of the first man he kills. The heads of all enemies killed in battle are taken to the king; if he brings a head, a soldier is admitted to his share of the loot; no head, no loot.*

A small table made from the scar tissue of a birch, on which lay a piece of mutton the size of a fist.

An Android smart phone set to vibrate.

A larger wooden table with a piece of horsemeat skewered by a bronze knife.

A wooden stirrer and some remains of koumiss or yogourt.

Herodotus: *He strips the skin off the head by making a circular cut round the ears and shaking out the skull; he then scrapes the flesh off the skin with the rib of an ox, and when it is clean works it in his fingers until it is supple, and fit to be used as a sort of handkerchief. He hangs these handkerchiefs on the bridle of his horse, and is very proud of them. The best man is the man who has the greatest number.*

The Telegraph, 8 AM GMT 03 Feb 2013: *Google Glass, the web giant's augmented reality spectacles, create sound by sending vibrations directly through the wearer's skull.*

Bits of gold foil from the ornamental carvings of her headdress that gleamed like tea lights in her dark coffin.

Charcoal-grey rain jacket with hood.

Hip-length white felt stockings.

A pair of jeans. Leather boots with a broken zipper.

A skirt with horizontal woven bands of maroon and white.

A skin of lake ice melting in the late-morning sun.

On the Pender bus this afternoon, a woman's hands
shiny and creased as rice paper. *Hold on, we're moving.*
An unwashed body and urine somewhere near me, in my
mouth, in my throat.

A memory stick. 512 MB. Made in China.

Burnt coriander.

Herodotus: *Many Scythians sew a number of scalps together and make cloaks out of them, like the ones peasants wear, and often, too, they take the skin, nails and all, off the right hands and arms of dead enemies and use it to cover their quivers with — having discovered the fact that human skin is not only tough, but white, as white as almost any skin.*

Radio Free Europe/Radio Liberty Photo of the Week, May 13, 2013: *Human skull is seen during the exhumation of a Stalin-era mass grave at the military cemetery in the heart of the Polish capital, Warsaw. The grave is believed to contain the remains of around 200 victims of a postwar campaign of communist terror.*

A vessel of horn, *translucent against the sun.* A fracture line where it had been broken and mended.

How light spilled over the blue-rimmed steppe at dawn.

How rain falls in the night.

Click of beads at her wrist.

2 June, 7 pm, at the Mount Pleasant Library. Notebook and papers before me. Flickering shadows of cyclists on Main in late sunlight.

Clink of metal bucket at dusk. Spill of water.

Red cloth case placed by her left thigh.

Hand mirror of polished metal.

Starry tattooed night.

IV.
GHOST

3 June. Some days I want to turn to you and ask if you remember the night we stood at the crossroads in Mojave City and listened to the train come in across the desert floor.

Thin line of steel piercing a vein. The rushing wind.

☙

3 June. Or, the Portuguese soup in Mike's café? Later, in the soft evening heat, we drove past the RV park and the boneyard. The broken aircraft you identified easily. Your language of frequencies and code. Our first date, you taught me how to tune in the shortwave at the Amateur Radio Society. BBC World Service. Deutsche Welle.

How the continent opened at night to AM waves refracted in the ionosphere. The radio dial's glow. Your fingers calling down voices—Art Bell drawn through static. Men talking conspiracies and angels.

℃

3 June. I have a book from that road trip—*100 Desert Wildflowers.* You always followed me where I wanted to go. Long Beach and a campsite in the dunes. A detour to a Portland bookstore. Hours drinking black coffee in the café, while I lost myself in books. You found it difficult to read. I always wanted more from you. I have no letter written in your hand. No photograph.

☙

CALTROP

41. Caltrop

Often abundant on road shoulders and in low spots where rainwater from hot-weather showers provides adequate moisture, caltrop or "summerpoppy," with large blossoms and attractive compound leaves, decorates the desert when other flowers are noticeable by their absence. The long, weak stems, usually prostrate, give the plants a vine-like appearance, but when growing under shrubs they extend upward so that the shrub is mistakenly thought to be blooming. Superficially resembling the springtime goldpoppy, caltrop has five rather than four petals, and may be found in bloom as late as October.

Kallstroemia grandiflora   Caltrop Family

3 June. At lunch, I sit next to a man in the cafeteria who tells me he sees a tattoo as what is left behind, as a trace of a process or event, just as a scar remembers a cut: the point where the blade entered the body, the story it tells.

☞

The tattooing...could be done either by stitching or by pricking in order to introduce a black colouring substance, probably soot, under the skin. The method of pricking is more likely than sewing, although the Altaians of this time had very fine needles and thread with which to have executed this. In the preparation of clothes of exceptionally fine squirrel and sable skin, as we have seen, minute stitches were passed through the material from the inside. Sinew thread was used only in the most superficial skin layer and never taken through to the external furry side. The considerable depth of the colouring substance in the body inclines one to the view that the tattooing was done not by sewing but by pricks.

☙

I look everywhere for you. In tins and shoeboxes.

There are so many things I cannot find.

A reel-to-reel with your name on the label
gummed to its centre, and a question mark.

Is it you?

I cut up your voice in C-control. Slip
the tape back and forth across the heads
to isolate a word, a breath
caught in the throat.

Meaning poured out of sound.

Slice it out. Tape it back again.

I can't recall your face, your voice.

Tape your tongue.

How much I missed of you.

Tape your lips.

ભ

4 June. As she emerged from the ice, toward the very end, they used their fingers to work at the fabric on her body, to ease her left arm out without tearing off her skin.

Her clasped hands, so.

In this way it felt as if she were coming to life beneath their fingertips.

So I work your body in memory.

These barbaric methods.

ભ

4 June. They used cupfuls of hot water, to slow the spill of tiny artifacts.

☙

5 June. But I resist. I approach you sideways. A little at a time, over years. I write a line and score it out. Write another line. Delete it.

෬

5 June. You recorded everything: the Dopplering train whistle and the insects that woke at dusk. The man at the gas station who taught us how to say *Tehachapi.* The wind against the sides of the van where we sheltered at night.

You tell me, *Listen.* You take my head in your hands, adjust my earphones, check the levels. A single insect, then a second, begins to sing. A chorus. Electric. This blue light. One group signalling to another across the high desert plain.

A train whistle approaches through the dusk. Enters me.

☙

Two pieces of string
on her little finger —

remember.

ः

5 June. The creosote and sage are taller than I imagined—to my waist, to my neck, like wading into a sea. The leaves flicker grey-green. You touch my arm to point out the Stealth bomber—an obsidian arrowhead that vanishes as you speak.

On the shoulder of Highway 58, a souvenir stall's mesh awning casts a shifting geometric veil across my arms, my wrists, your olive skin, your blunt fingertips. You buy me a keychain—a stoppered vial of blue liquid that fades eventually and leaks out of the plastic tube, leaving only the blanched alien embryo with its almond eyes.

Her people, known from historical sources as cruel nomads, had excellent weapons, such as the double curved bow made of horn and strung with sinew, arrows tipped with stone, bronze, iron or bone, swords, short daggers, celts, axes and picks, and sometimes lances.

೮ʑ

The skin is inscribed. This is not metaphor but *actual material modification of flesh through cutting, piercing, painting, or tattooing.* This is the body as *being in the world.*

The skin is inscribed. This is metaphor. *Perceptions and memories are entangled inside and through the body's surface.*

CB

6 June. A strange patchwork. Your hair so black it looked dyed. Scuffed brown loafers and a wine velour sweater you wore innocently. A languor in your stride. I don't remember how you taste. I don't remember your chest, your ears, your thighs.

ᚙ

44. Samija mentzelia

There are many kinds of mentzelia, all herbs found in the West. The barbed hairs which cover the stems and leaves cause the plant to cling to whatever it touches, giving it the common name "stick-leaf." Flowers grow at the ends of the branches and some species open fully only in sunlight. *Mentzelia involucrata*, also called "sand blazing star," is an annual, 4 to 16 inches high, found in hot sandy washes below 3,000 feet in southwestern Arizona, southeastern California, and northern Sonora. It blooms from February through April. One variety, *megalantha*, has larger brighter, yellower flowers than the typical *involucrata*.

Mentzelia involucrata   Loasa Family

6 June. The train is far out on the desert floor. We stand at the crossing, silent, because you are recording. My head fits under your collarbone. The train's thin whistle spools itself within the Marantz, laying down a ghostly track that will remain long after your body shielding mine is ash.

∞

Provisions for life after death:

Remove the eyes.

Remove the teeth—*seeds of life.*

Remove the wet membranes.

Remove the cartilage of the ribs.

Anoint the head and the skin with resin, with oil, with beeswax.

Clothing is the receptacle for the soul.
Clothe the body in plain weave and twill, T-shirt and denim.

Prepare vessels of clay, of horn, of wood.

Pour a drink for the gods.

Smoke a cigarette.

CR

91. Whitestem paperflower

At its best in sandy desert soil, paperflower is a compact, shrubby plant about 1 foot high, with tangled branches. When fully developed it is symmetrically globular in outline. It prefers mesas and desert plains at elevations between 2,000 and 5,000 feet from western New Mexico to southern California and northern Mexico, flowering throughout the year but most abundantly in springtime. Sometimes called "paper-daisy," the flowers are persistent, fading to straw color and turning papery with age. They may remain on the stems for weeks.

Psilostrophe cooperi   Sunflower Family

WHITESTEM PAPERFLOWER

77

Techniques employed in working the different materials:

I remove the skin and work it with my fingers to make it soft
and pliable. I thread a needle with sinew and run the line
beneath the most translucent layer. I make small stitches.
I patch the damaged places. I mix ash with red wine to
make a paste. I draw letters with the tip of my finger on
the inside of your thigh. I sharpen my knife and make small
cuts in a circular fashion. I scoop out the marrow. I make
perforations and join them with strands of hemp. I inspect
the fibres for swellings and thickenings. I plait the words.
I bind your wrists. I mark you with ash. I mark you with
ochre and cinnabar. I soften you with my fingertips.

ജ

7 June. I know more of her burial site than yours.

I place you here—in the Mojave.

In this sere blue.

V.
BLUE
ACROSS THIS
LAND THAT
LOOKS LIKE
SEA

The steppe is said to have a *glacial memory.*

In this way, it was dreaming her, as I do.

⳩

12 June. Some of the archaeologists had nightmares. Eyes hooked from their skulls. Bodies rising from the earth, skin imprinted with blades of grass or flowers. Some interpreted these dreams as signs they were not meant to be there— that Ledi herself was telling them to go. In the daylight, in the weak summer sunlight of the steppe, she lay pinned under white gauze.

‿‿

Do not shout—it is a sacrilege—do not offend the spirits
in this second layer of heaven, *the end of everything.*

☙

12 June. There is a biochemistry to the body's decay
after death. It begins in the gut with autolysis, as micro-
organisms in the stomach's lining that once helped to digest
food now consume the body itself. They travel through the
veins, the arteries, to the brain, the lungs, the heart. This
process had been arrested in Ledi, her cavities scraped out
and filled with earth and dried grasses. Then ice preserved
her for millennia.

Steppe fescue, couch grass, steppe oat, wild oat, spear grass
and so many small flowers in the spring.

CR

13 June. Coming out to the university on the 99 B-Line, I pull on the hood of my rain jacket against the blank morning light. Drops of rain slip through the open window and soak into the page of my book:

In early spring, when the Iris, Altai anemone and campion are flowering, the ground is covered by a blue-grey carpet; in summer, the varied steppe-meadow grasses flower luxuriantly; and finally in the early autumn, wormwood and feather grass.

଼

13 June. Her decay began the moment her skin came into contact with human hands and sunlight, with tiny micro-organisms in the warmed lake water used to melt the ice. Her skin darkened with mould like a page as it burns. She was taken by helicopter to Novosibirsk, where she might be better preserved.

Apply the colour blue to an object and it will reduce, cut open, and destroy its shape....Movement and sound, like shapes, disappear into blue, sink and vanish like a bird in the sky. Insubstantial in itself, blue disembodies whatever becomes caught in it.

☙

13 June. Although it is not known when she died, she was buried in the second half of June, when the earth had thawed enough to dig. The incisions on her body show where she was cut open to remove her vital organs, her lungs, her womb, and then sewn back up with braided horsehair thread. The cavities were packed with peat moss and bark, rich in tannin, to preserve her from decay.

As blue darkens, *it becomes the colour of dreams. Conscious thought yields little by little to the unconscious, just as the light of day gradually becomes the light of night, midnight blue.*

☙

14 June. Once, after I had moved to Montreal, I wrote to him to ask whether radio waves travel forever. He wrote back from South Africa, and said that some radio waves, in the form of electromagnetic radiation, are held in place on the earth by the layers of atmosphere. But some slip through and travel forever away from the earth, becoming fainter and fainter, still there, barely detectable, travelling through the vastness of the universe.

CR

How do we measure the dimensions of a human body?

By the major elements—oxygen, carbon, hydrogen, nitrogen, calcium, phosphorous.

By the minor elements—potassium, sulphur, sodium, chlorine, magnesium.

By the trace elements—cobalt, selenium, lead.

By materials and tissues—muscle, fat, bone, lymph, blood.

By molecular type—DNA, free radicals, nucleotides.

Stresses and fractures.

Scars, scores.

Time.

CR

15 June. The helicopter was delayed by an early snowstorm. They woke to a blinding whiteness that lasted three days. On August 7 the helicopter arrived. They had already filled the kurgan and broken camp. Ninety miles from Novosibirsk an engine died and the helicopter began to spin at 3,000 feet until the pilot at last gained control and landed in a farmer's field. A truck took them the final distance to Novosibirsk, where Ledi was placed in a laboratory freezer.

The methods used by Russian biochemists to halt her decay were the same ones used to preserve the body of Lenin.

CR

15 June. We know when she was buried because of the larvae of the horsefly *Gastrophilus intestinalis* found in the sacrificed horses, and because of the flowers in the roof of the kurgan, which only blossom at the end of June.

CR

15 June. Perhaps this is how it was for her:

Clink of a metal bucket at dusk.

Tap of hammers, scrape of rock on rock.

Sluice of water.

Melting ice like gentle taps of rain.

First light.

ॐ

Like a bone needle that punctures your skin to inscribe a line of ink, to be with another is to allow them to enter into you, through cartilage and nerve and blood, until you are suffused with them, and permanently marked.

CR

Steppe fescue, couch grass, steppe oat, wild oat, spear grass.

Yellow oat grass, feather grass, cat's paw. Wild garlic, Iris ruthenica.

☙

Meadow ragwort, iris root, cyclamen. Holy wormwood, campion.

⚇

NOTES

Archaeologists believe that the Pazyryks were closely related to the Scythians, described by Herodotus in his *Histories*. The Altai people, who live today in the Ukok Plateau, have called repeatedly for the reburial of Ledi, whom they identify as an ancestor.

Italicized quotations woven throughout the book are drawn from the following sources: Natalya Polosmak, "Siberian Mummy Unearthed," *National Geographic,* October 1994, and "The Burial of a Noble Pazyryk Woman," *Ancient Civilizations from Scythia to Siberia,* 1998; Rima Eriknova, director of the Altay Regional Museum in Gorno-Altaysk, speaking in the 2010 BBC documentary *Scythian Ice Maiden*; Enid Schildkrout, "Inscribing the Body," *Annual Review of Anthropology,* vol.33, 2004; Sergei Rudenko, *Frozen Tombs of Siberia* (University of California Press, 1970); Francis Van Noten and Natalya Polosmak, "The Frozen Tombs of the Scythians," *Endeavour,* 1995; the entry for "blue" in *The Penguin Dictionary of Symbols*; Herodotus, *The Histories*, translated by Aubrey de Sélincourt and John Marincola (Penguin, 1964).

Illustrations in "Ghost" are from Natt N. Dodge, *100 Desert Wildflowers in Natural Color* (Southwest Parks and Monuments Association, 1963).

ACKNOWLEDGEMENTS

The first draft of *Ledi* was written in the learning commons of what used to be the old main library at the University of British Columbia, and in the Mount Pleasant library in East Van, on the traditional, ancestral, unceded territories of the xʷməθkwəy̓əm, Skwxwú7mesh, and Səl̓ílwətaʔ/Selilwitulh Nations. I also gratefully acknowledge the Canada Council for providing me with a writer's grant and a travel grant.

Part IV, "Ghost," was written during my participation in the Banff Writing Studio in May 2016. I'd like to thank the Banff Centre for Arts and Creativity, situated on the traditional territory of the Stoney Nakoda, Blackfoot, and Tsuut'ina Nations, for providing this time and place, and the poetry faculty: Karen Solie, for encouraging me to take "Ghost" through a third draft, and for her close line by line reading of the entire book; Lisa Robertson, for contextualizing *Ledi* in terms of Mallarmé's genre of the tombeau; and Michael Dickman, for syntax. My fellow poets at Banff provided an intense experience. In particular, I'd like to thank Julie Joosten for her calm strength and friendship, and Jennifer Zilm, who annotated "Ghost" one long Tuesday as we wrote in the Old Banff Cemetery.

Thanks to my first readers, Kristie Trainor and Tom Playfair. Noah Quastel read the poem from a Marxist human geographer's perspective and corrected some inaccuracies in the flora of the Endowment lands. Yudel Huberman was my touchstone. My thanks to Kate Hargreaves for her beautiful cover design, to my editor Jennifer LoveGrove for her generous, discerning guidance in my final excavation of the text, and to Stuart Ross for the fine details. A heartfelt thanks to Jay and Hazel at Book*hug.

This book is for Stefan.